Soccer Coloring Book For Kids

Published in 2024 by The Future Teacher Foundation

© The Future Teacher Foundation 2024

www.thefutureteacherfoundation.com

ISBN-13: 9798878321099

For printing and manufacturing information please see the last page.

All images copyright © The Future Teacher Foundation 2024

No part of this publication may be reproduced, stored in a retrieval system, or transmitted, in any form or by any means, electronic, mechanical, photocopying, recording, or otherwise, without the prior permission of the publishers

If you choose to remove pages for framing, ask an adult to carefully extract with a scalpel and ruler.

Warning: This book is not suitable for children under 36 months of age due to potential small parts - choking hazard.

This book belongs to...

_____

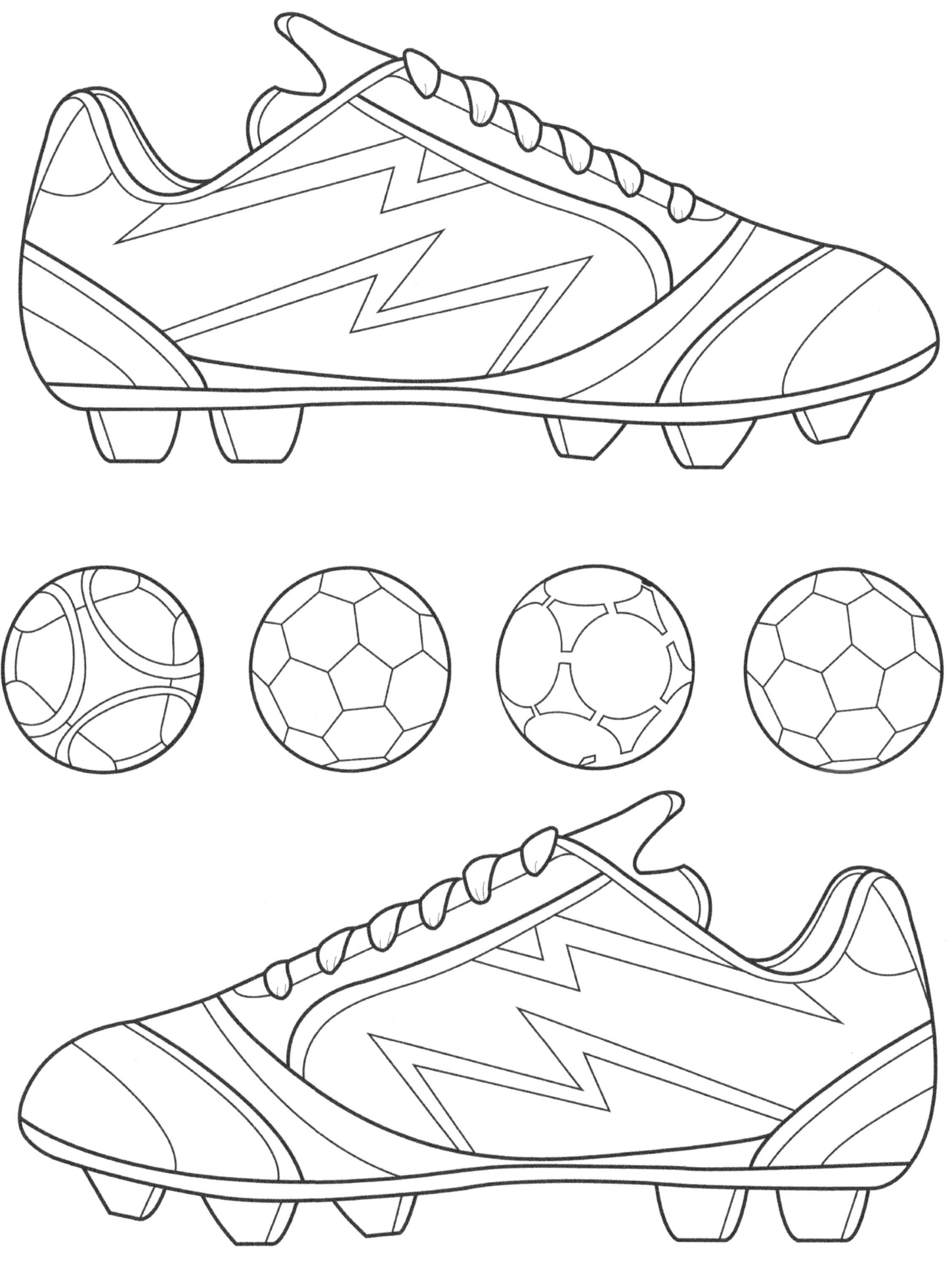

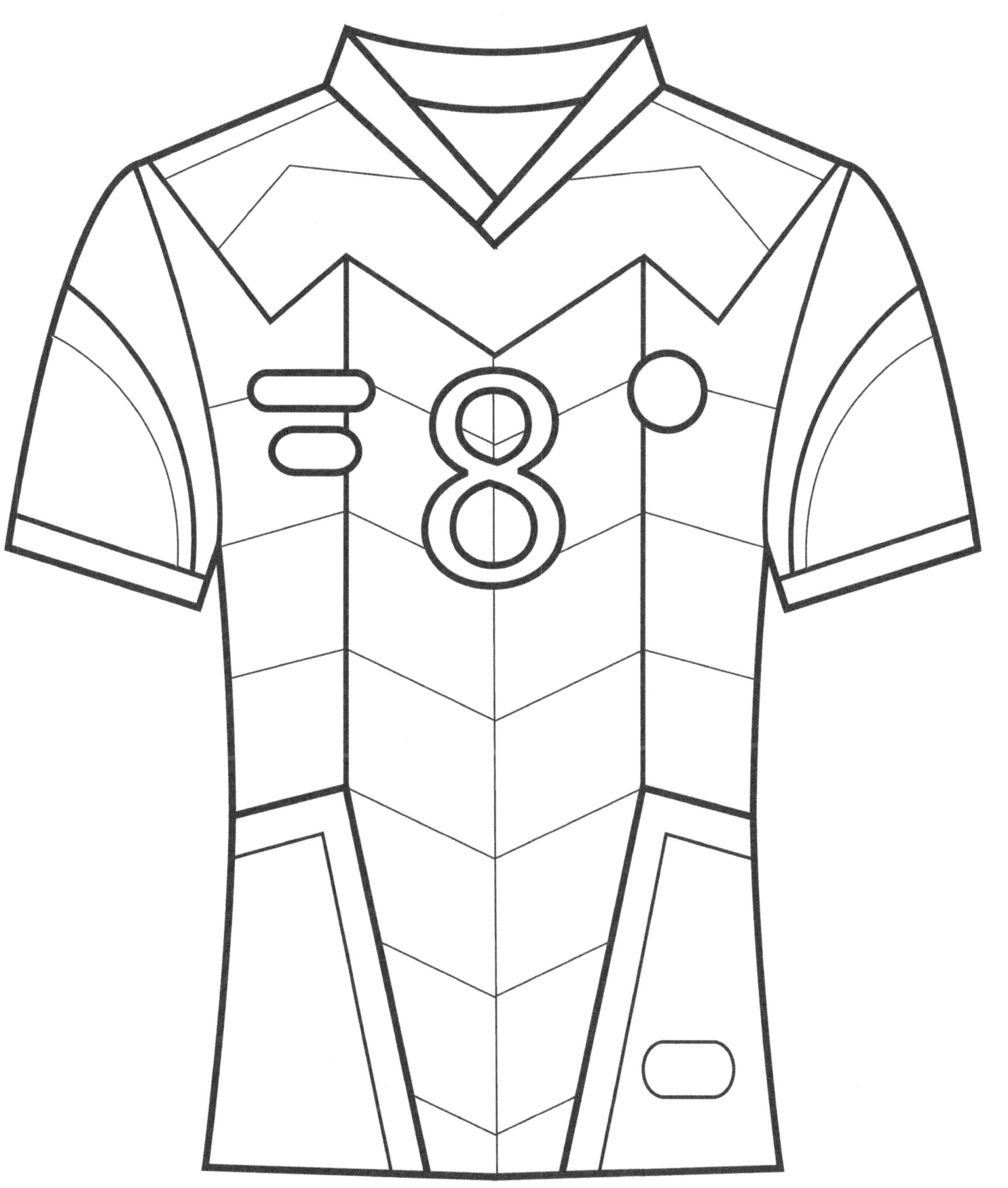

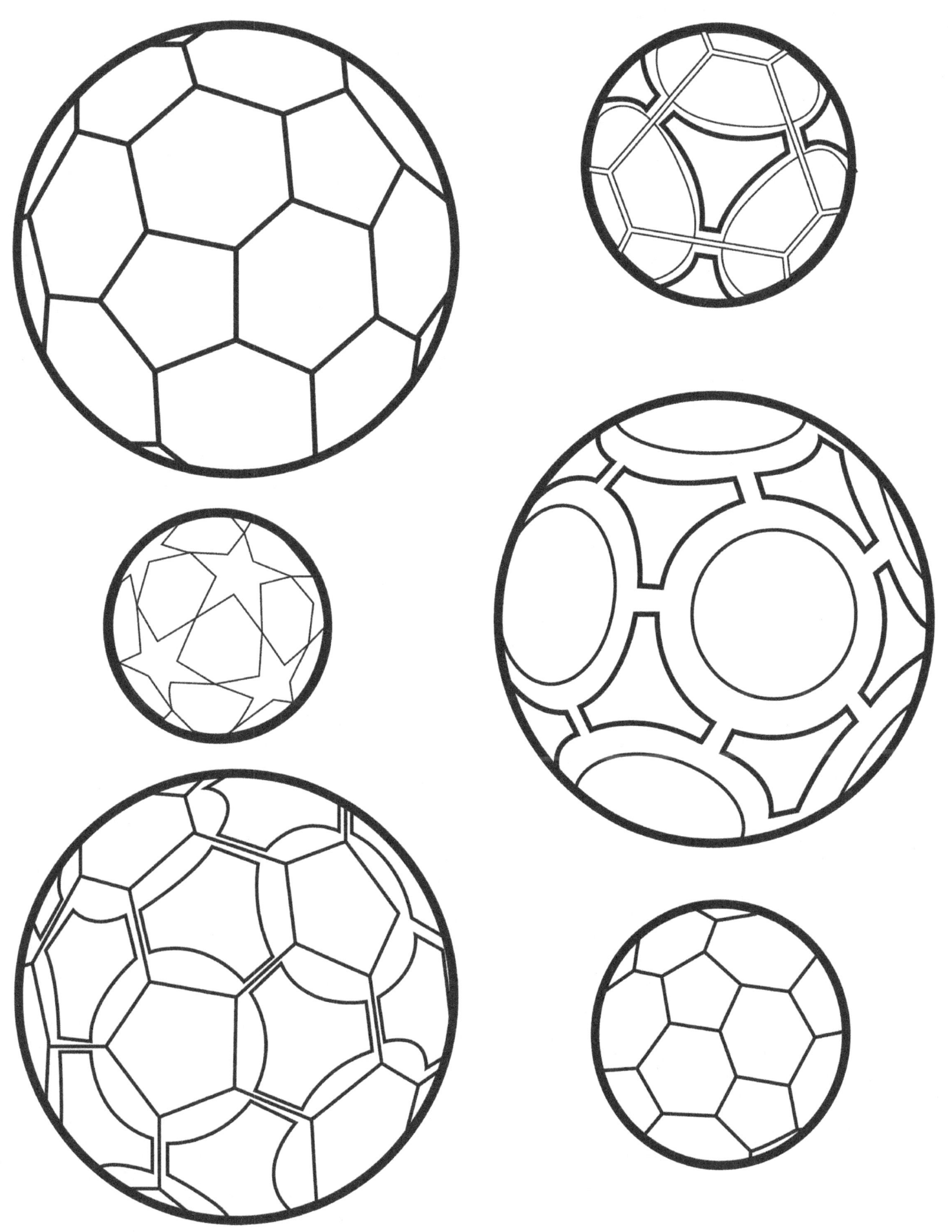

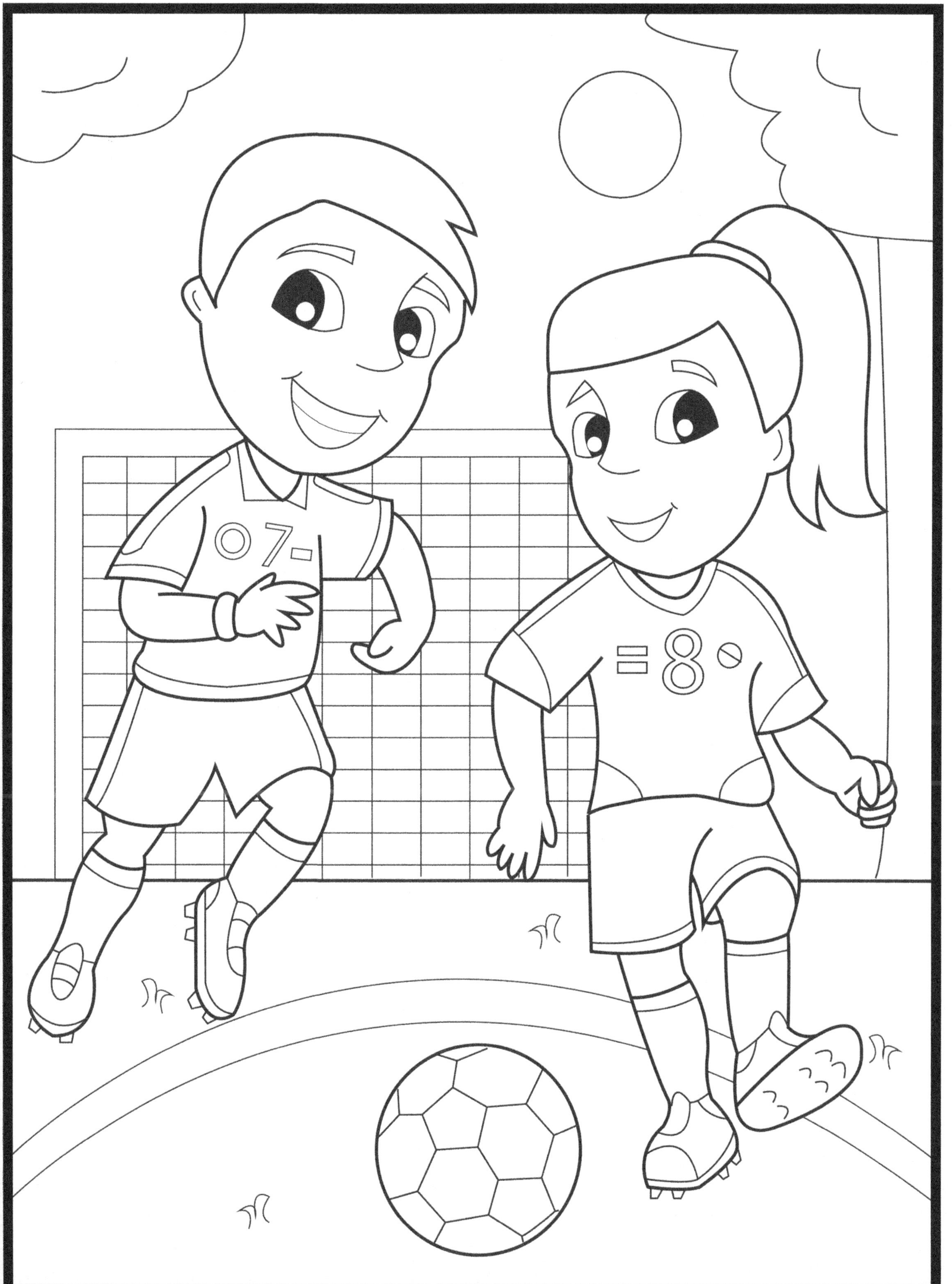
07
8

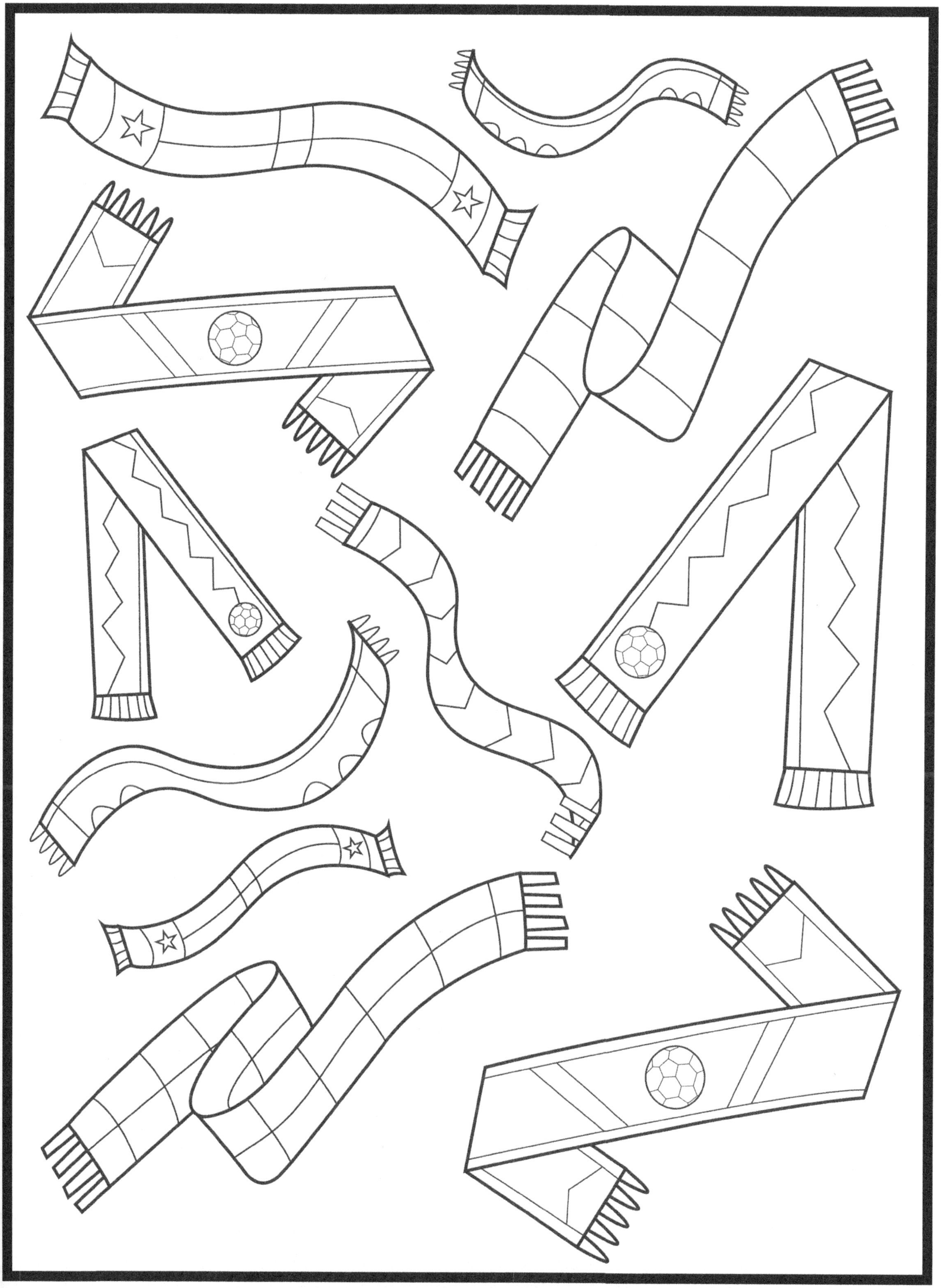

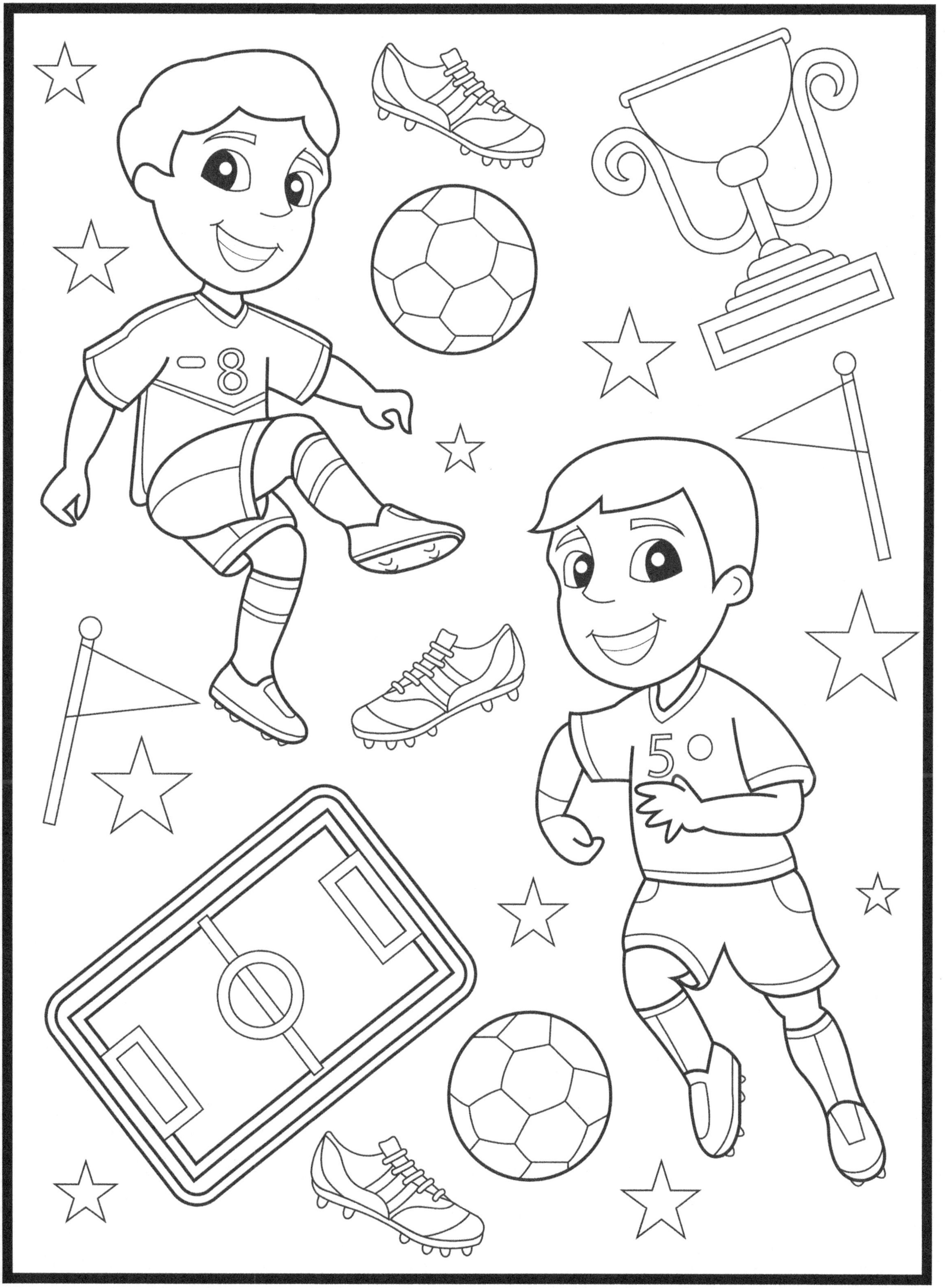
8
5

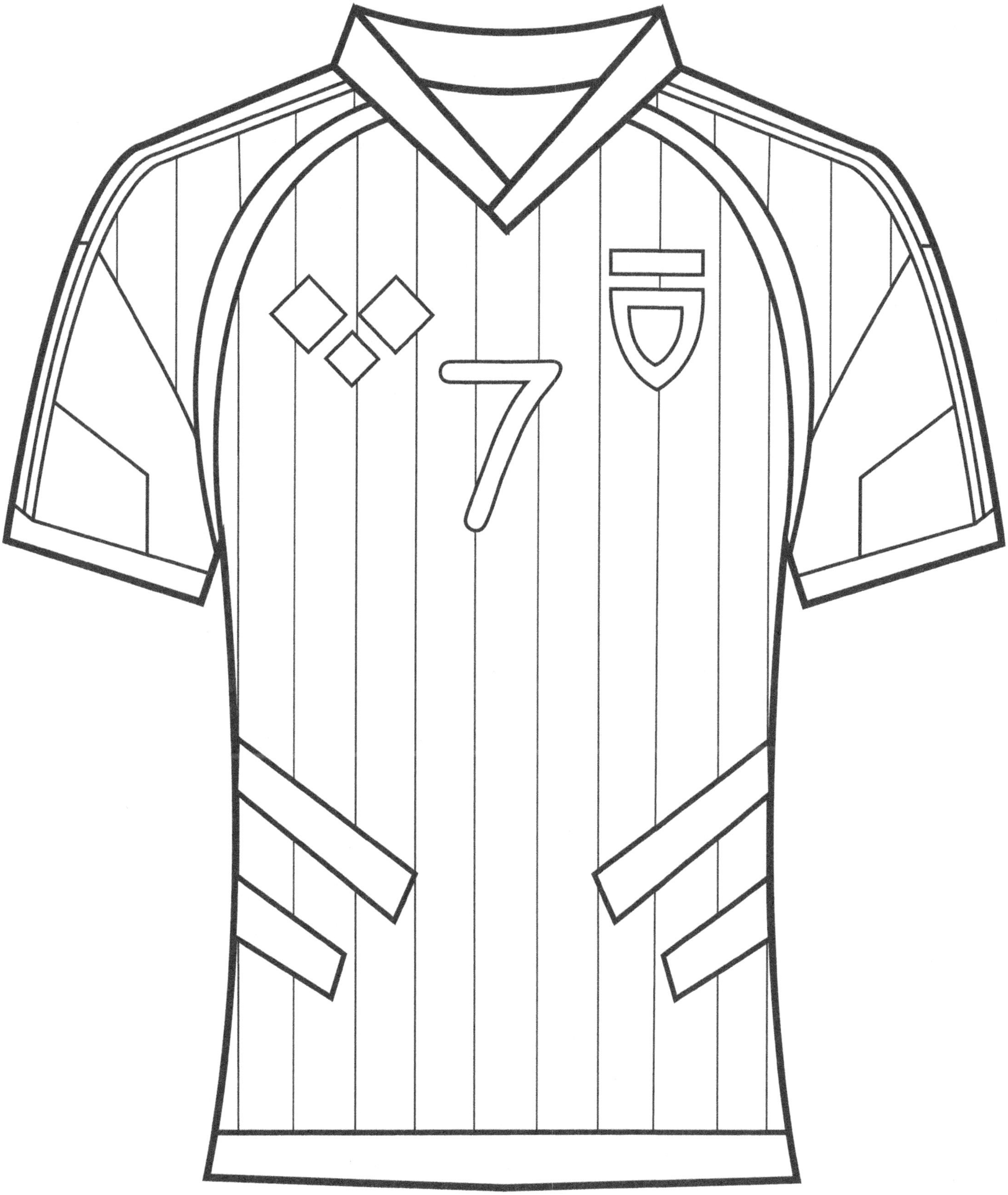
7

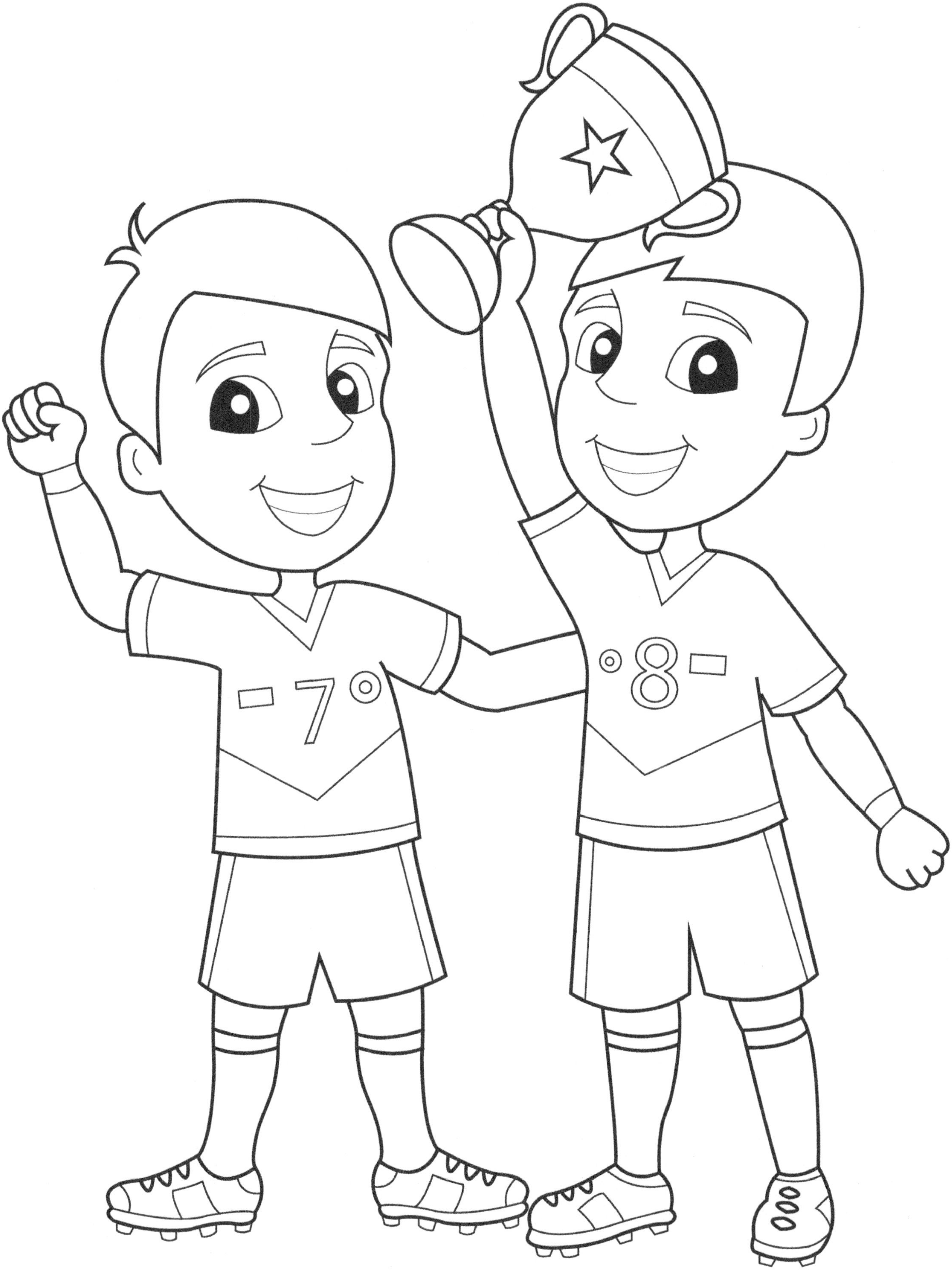
7
8

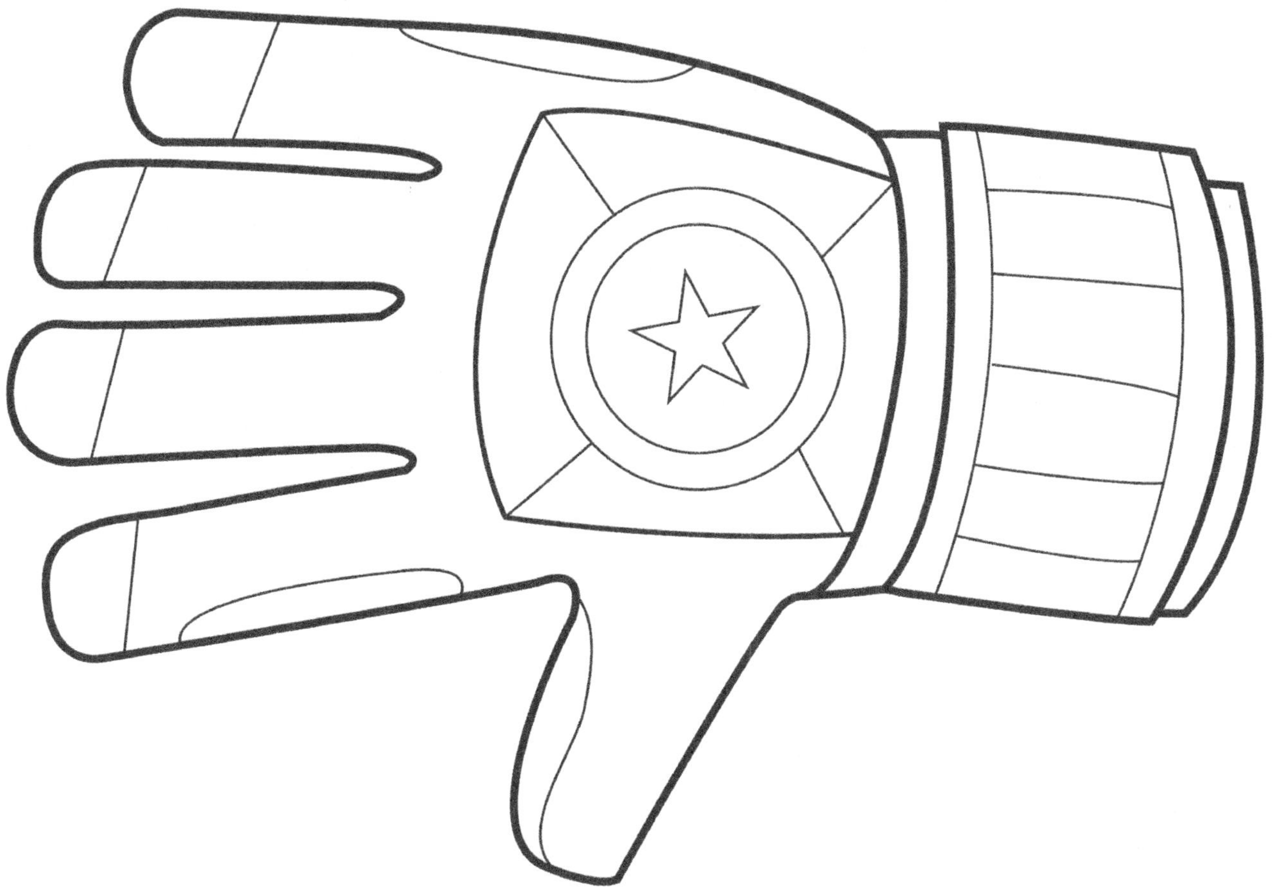

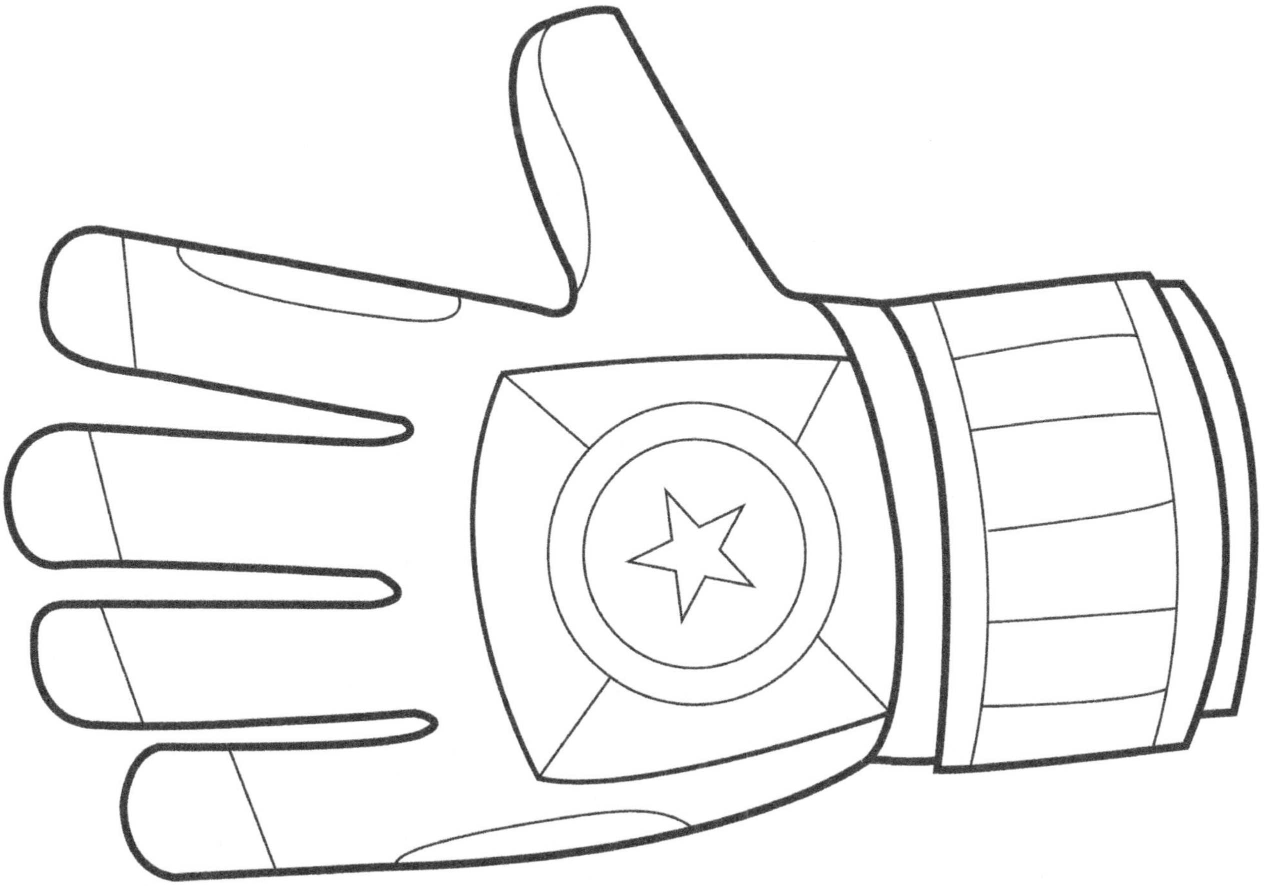

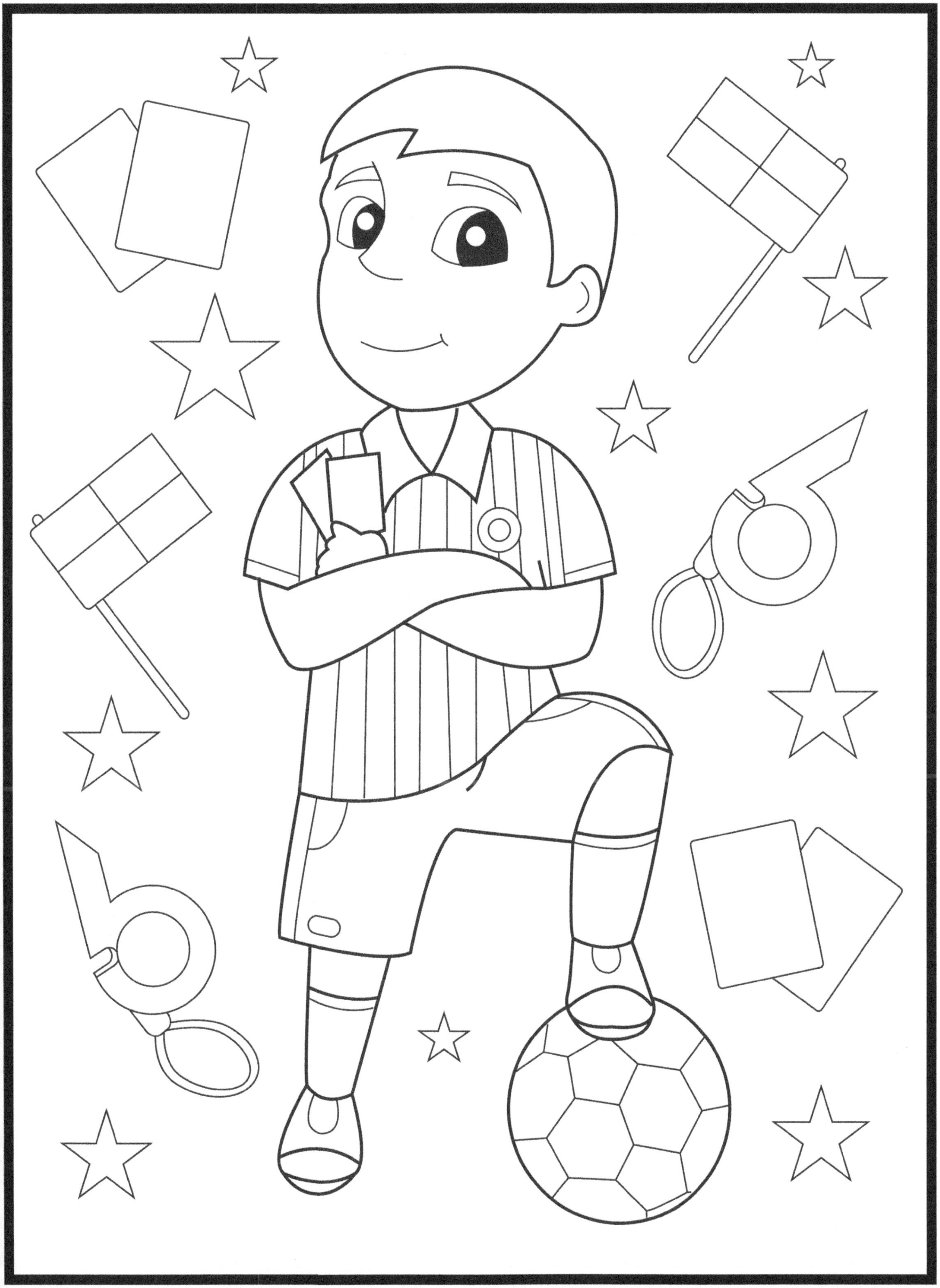

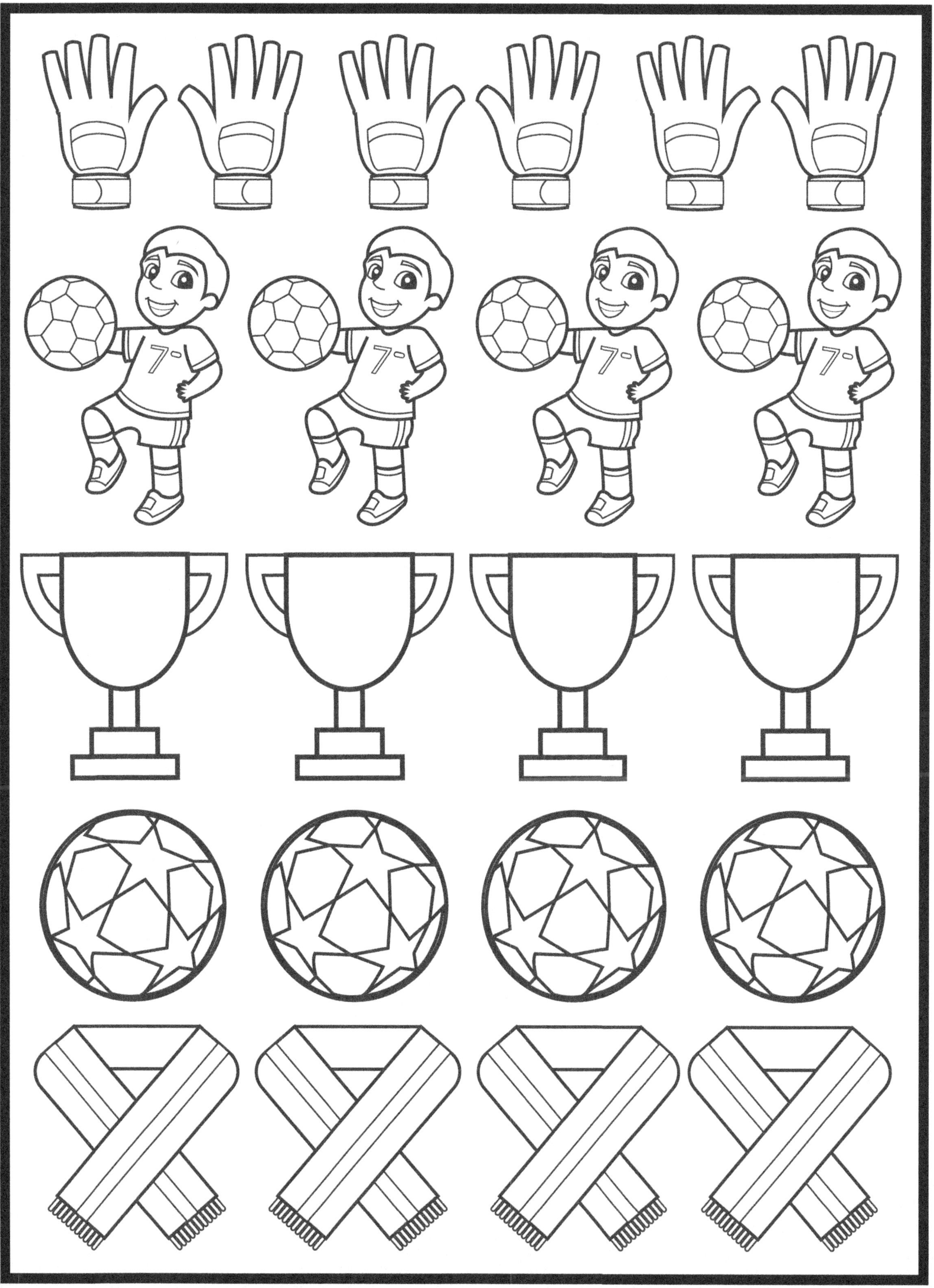
7
7
7
7

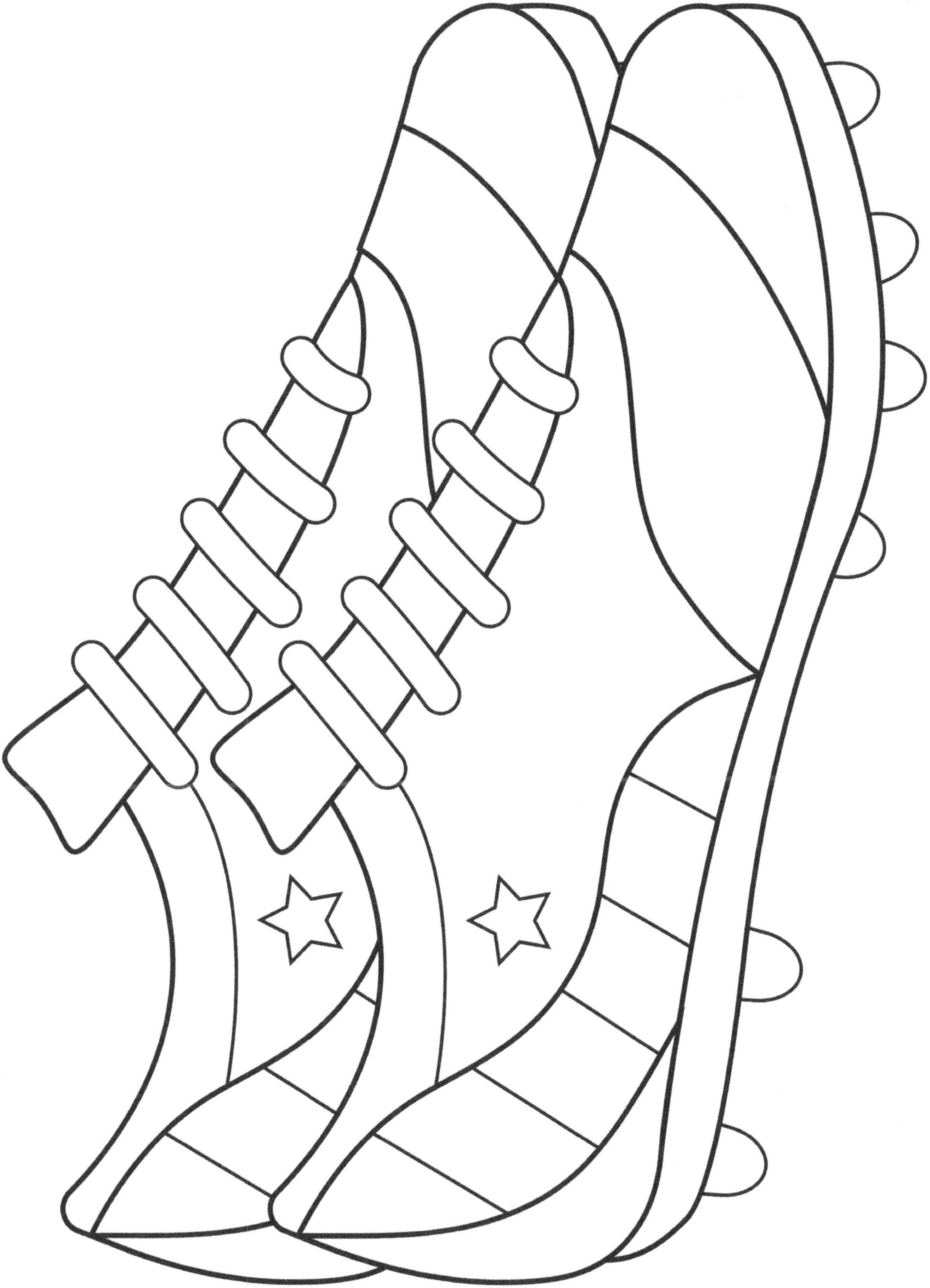

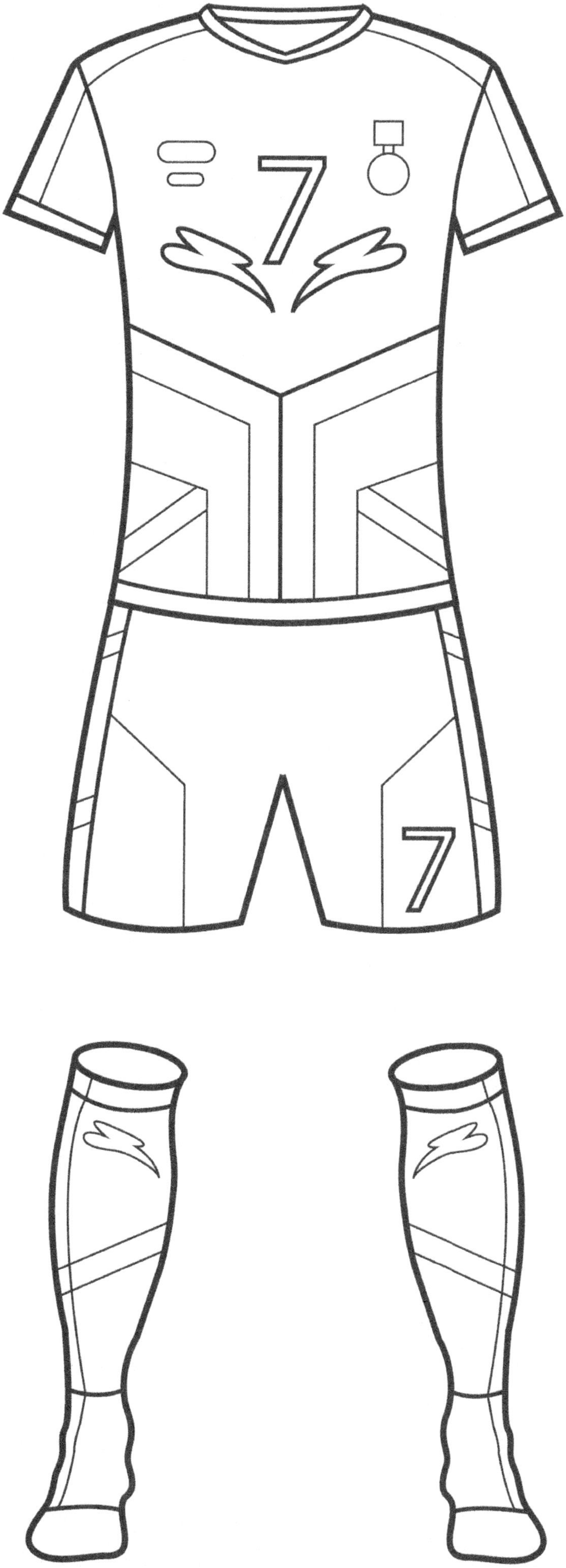
7
7

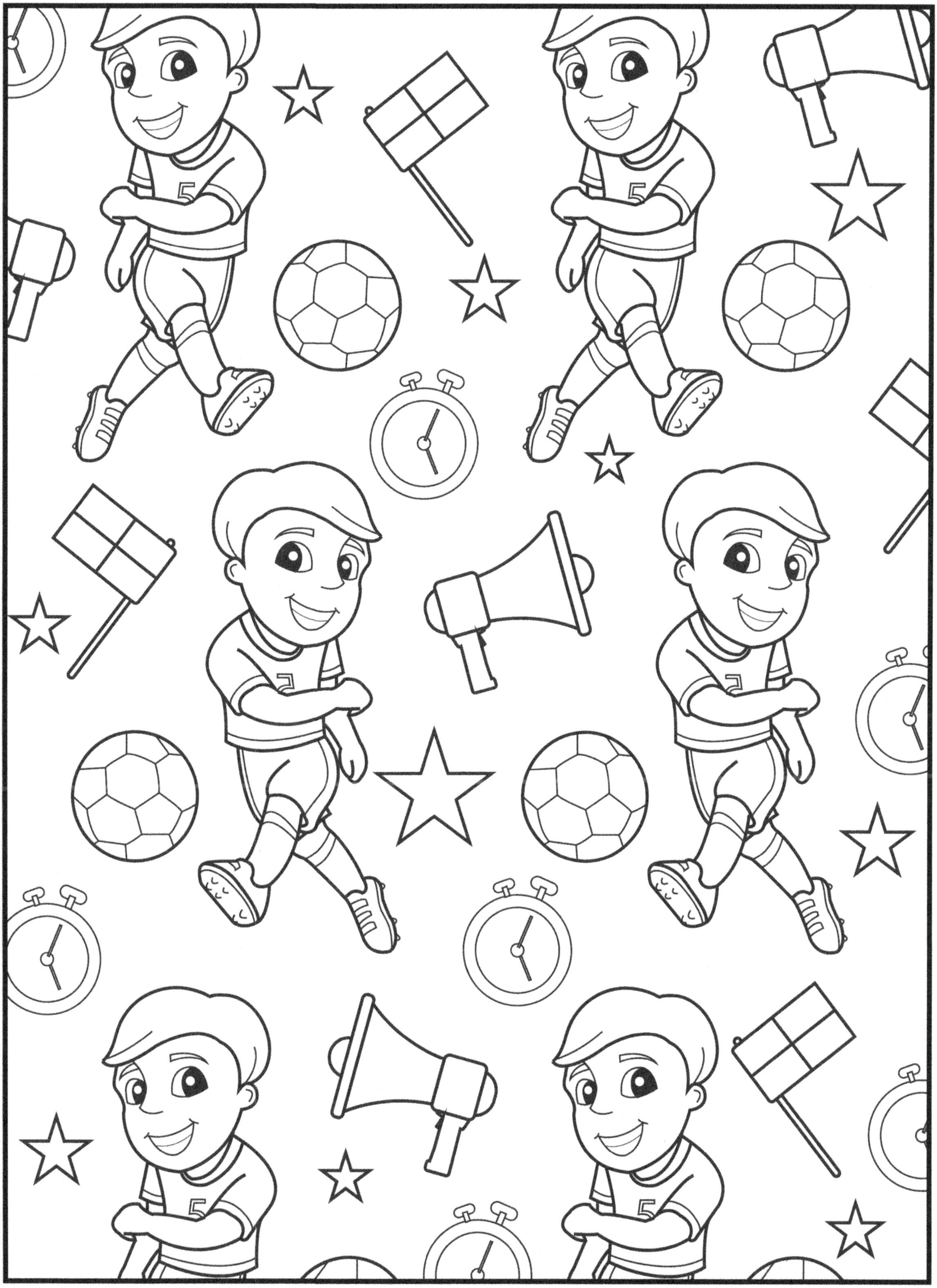

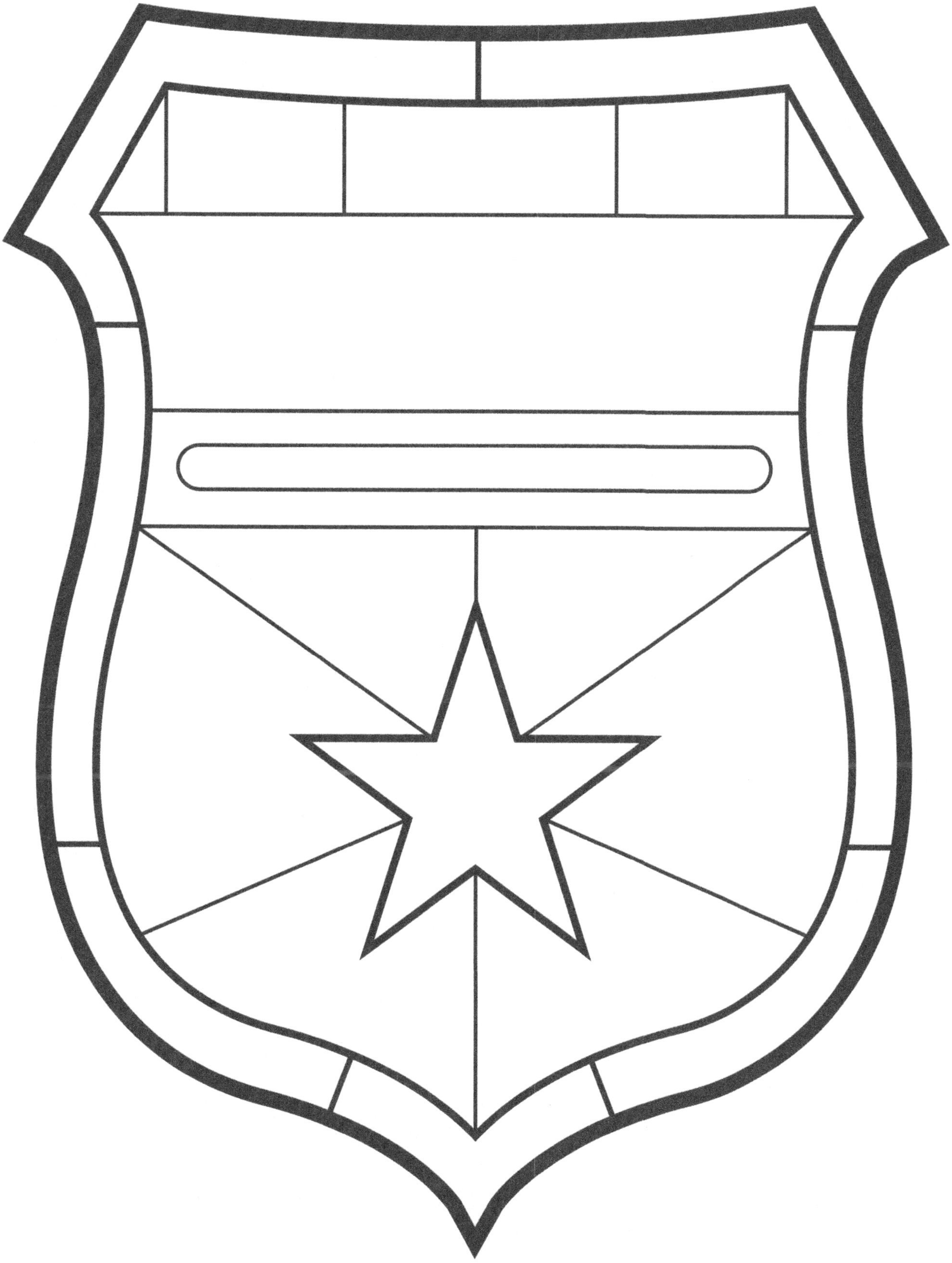

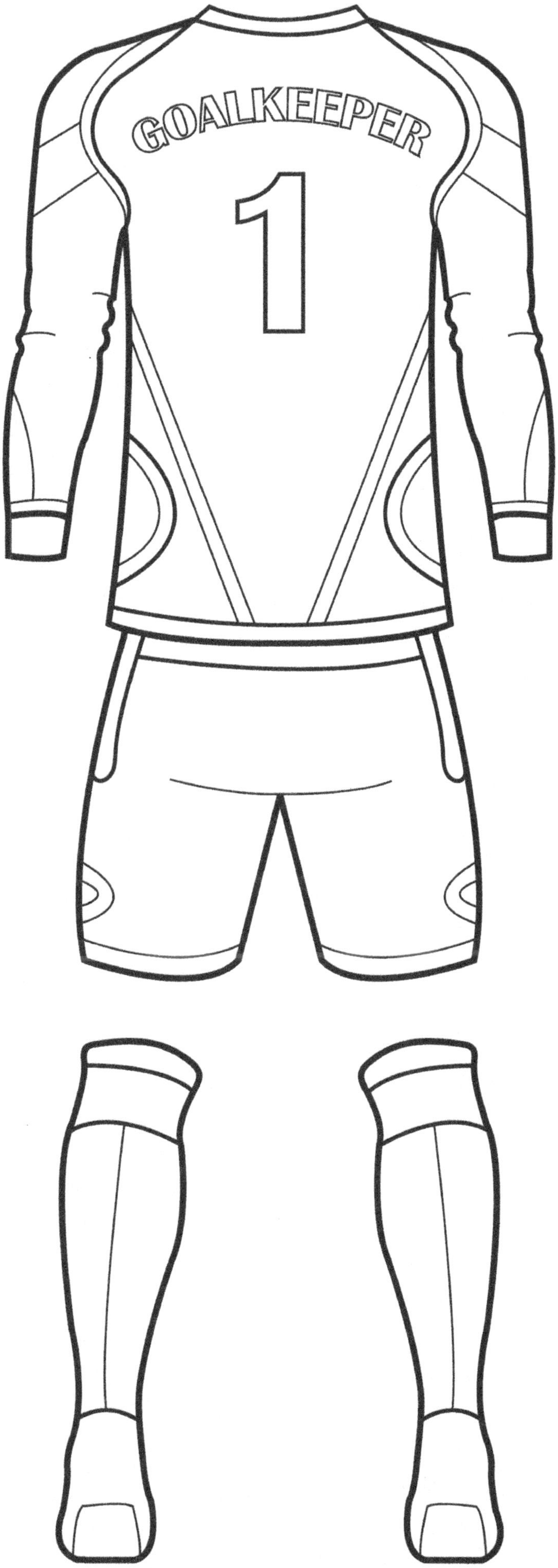
GOALKEEPER
1

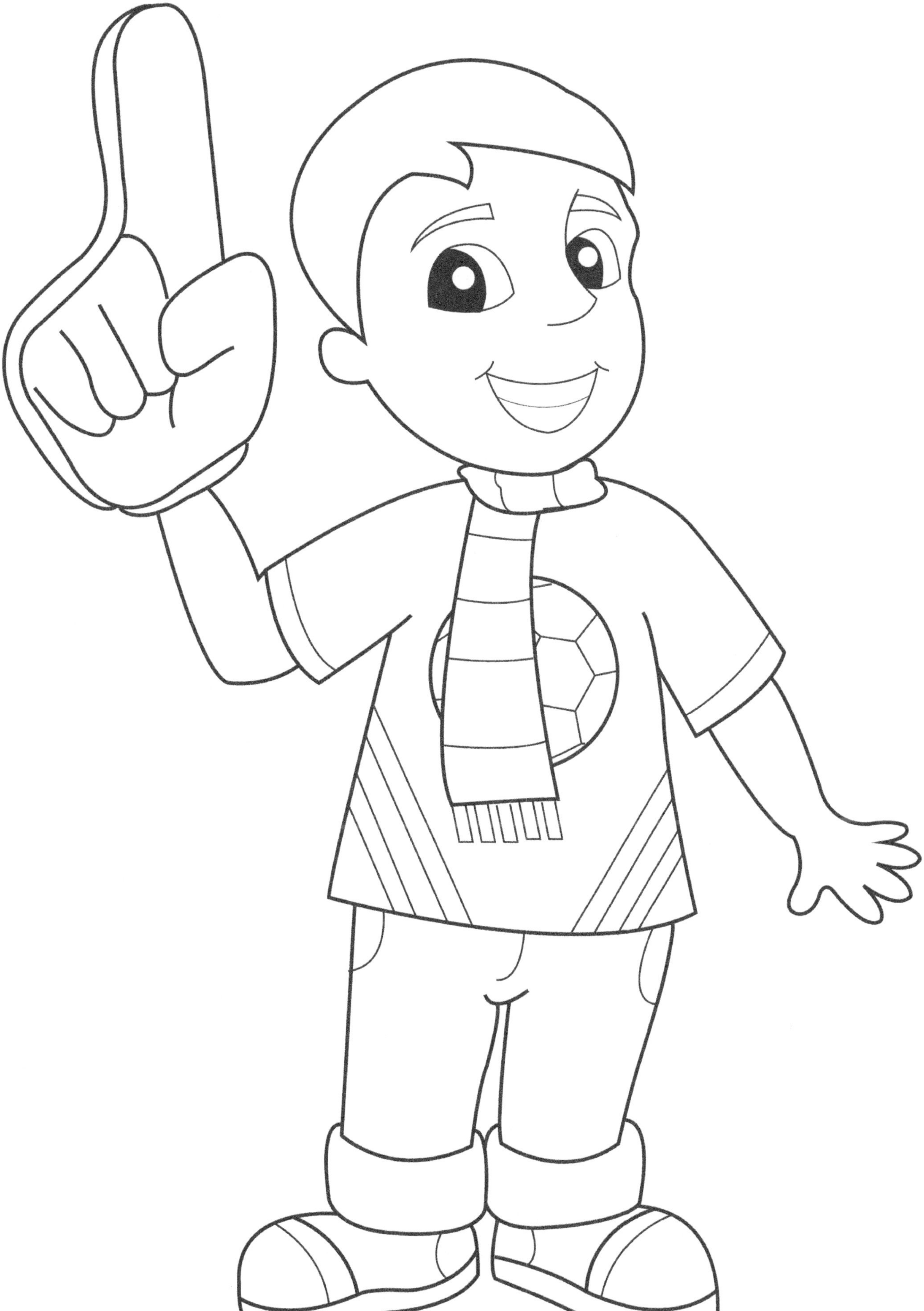

Made in United States
Orlando, FL
29 January 2025